PEOPLE & PLACES

Written by

Antony Mason

Consultant Dr. James Walvin

Illustrated by

Borin van Loon and Ann Savage

SILVER BURDETT PRESS
ENGLEWOOD CLIFFS, NEW JERSEY

U.S. Project Editor Nancy Furstinger
U.S. Editor Ruth Marsh
Editor Caroline White
Designer Robert Mathias, Publishing Workshop
Photo-researcher Hugh Olliff

A TEMPLAR BOOK

Devised and produced by Templar Publishing Co. Ltd.
Pippbrook Mill, London Road, Dorking, Surrey RH4 1JE

Adapted and first published in the United States in 1989
by Silver Burdett Press, Englewood Cliffs, N.J.

Color separations by Positive Colour Ltd, Maldon, Essex
Printed by L.E.G.O., Vicenza, Italy

Library of Congress Cataloging-in-Publication Data

Mason, Antony.
The Caribbean / Antony Mason. — 1st U.S. ed.
p. cm. — (People & places series)
Includes index.
Summary: Introduces the many islands of the Caribbean Sea.
1. Caribbean Area—Juvenile literature. [1. Caribbean Area.]
I. Title. II. Series: People & places (Englewood Cliffs, N.J.)
F2161.5.M37 1989
972.9—dc 19 89-4310
ISBN 0-382-09823-4 CIP
AC

Contents

ISLANDS IN THE SUN

The Caribbean is a chain of islands that borders the Caribbean Sea. They lie in a long, sweeping curve at the western end of the Atlantic Ocean between the two great land masses of North and South America.

To the north are the hundreds of little islands that make up the Bahamas. Below these are the largest islands of the region, which form a group called the Greater Antilles. These are Cuba, Jamaica, Puerto Rico, and the island of Hispaniola, which is divided into two countries, Haiti and the Dominican Republic.

South and east of Puerto Rico are the Lesser Antilles. These contain the two chains of islands called the Leeward Islands and the Windward Islands, as well as Trinidad and Tobago, Barbados, and the islands of the Netherlands Antilles, off the coast of Venezuela. The islands of the Greater and Lesser Antilles are also known as the West Indies.

There is a great variety in all these islands, not only in what they look like, but also in the people who live on them, their histories, their governments, and the languages the people speak. However, most of these islands have one thing in common — a painful, difficult, and often violent past.

KEY FACTS

- The Caribbean contains 13 independent countries and some 14 islands (or groups of islands) that are colonies, dependencies, or departments of European countries or the U.S.
- The total population of the Caribbean is about 30 million.
- None of the Caribbean countries is very wealthy. Haiti is one of the world's poorest countries.
- There is only one land border in the Caribbean, the one that separates Haiti from the Dominican Republic on the island called Hispaniola.
- The main languages are Spanish, English, and French, and local languages, or dialects, called creoles or patois. These dialects are based on European and African languages.
- Most of the major towns and cities of the region are ports.

Symbols of the Caribbean

Bougainvillea, with its billowing clumps of colored leaves, is one of the islands' most attractive plants.
The long, heavy knife, called by its Spanish name *machete*, is a familiar tool throughout the Caribbean. It is used mainly for cutting sugar cane, and also for opening fresh coconuts.

Island beauty

The warm seas and beautiful beaches of the Caribbean islands bring tourists from all over the world. Tourism is now one of the Caribbean's most important industries, and the sea also remains a vital source of food for many islanders.

Cuba

Cuba is by far the largest island. It also has the largest population, of more than 10 million. Havana, the capital, is the region's largest city, with more than one million inhabitants.

VOLCANOES AND CORAL

If you drained all the water out of the Atlantic Ocean, you would see that the Caribbean islands consist of the tips of huge mountains that rise from the sea bed.

The large islands of the Greater Antilles are part of a massive mountain range, and have the highest mountains in the region. Many of the islands of the Lesser Antilles are the jagged tips of ancient volcanoes. These hilly islands have plenty of rainfall and many rivers. The soil is fertile and produces lush green plants and forests.

Islands such as Barbados and Antigua rise from the limestone tops of undersea mountains. Others have been formed by massive banks of coral that have grown up in shallow water over thousands of years. These low-lying islands tend to be drier, with rains during the annual wet season.

In the Caribbean there is a wet season and a dry season. Throughout the year it is hot, with temperatures around 77°F. This is known as a tropical climate, for the Caribbean lies near the Tropic of Cancer, where the sun shines from directly overhead.

A famous disaster
On May 8, 1902 Mount Pelée on the island of Martinique in the Windward Islands erupted suddenly, sending a cloud of burning ash over the town of St. Pierre. This destroyed the town and killed the entire population of 40,000 people, except for one man. He was protected from the eruption by the thick walls of the prison where he was awaiting trial.

Although the volcano is still active, the modern town of St. Pierre has been rebuilt on the same site.

Steamy jungle
Higher land in the Caribbean is often shrouded in cloud. In many places the clouds bring heavy rain and tropical rain forests have developed on the hillsides beneath.

KEY FACTS

▶ The highest mountain in the Caribbean is the Pico Duarte in the Dominican Republic, which is 10,417 feet high.

▶ Only two of the volcanoes in the region are still active: Mount Pelée on Martinique, and Mount Soufrière on St. Vincent. Mount Soufrière last erupted in 1979.

▶ The deepest part of the Atlantic Ocean lies just to the east of Puerto Rico, and is 28,642 feet deep.

▶ The dry season usually lasts from around January to May or June; the wet season from May to November or December.

▶ Many of the volcanic islands have beaches of black sand, which forms from particles of black volcanic lava.

Tropical fury

The combination of a hot climate and vast expanses of ocean produces violent tropical hurricanes. These sweep in from the Atlantic between June and November, frequently causing widespread damage and numerous deaths. An average of six hurricanes occur every year. Shown here is the damage caused to a town in Jamaica by Hurricane Gilbert in 1988.

Microscopic builders

Coral is formed by tiny marine animals called polyps, which build casings of hard lime around themselves. Over thousands of years a mass of coral can form a reef, and eventually an island. Living undersea coral is beautifully colored and can take almost any shape. It is one of the great attractions for divers in the Caribbean.

NATURAL COLOR

The tropical climate and fertile soil of the Caribbean provide an excellent setting for a wide range of colorful wildlife.

Parrots live in the tropical forests, and flamingoes and scarlet ibises in the coastal marshlands. Tiny emerald-green hummingbirds dart around the bushes, sucking nectar from the numerous flowers of the islands, especially the large red, orange, or yellow Hibiscus flowers.

In the shallow parts of the sea thousands of beautiful fish glint in the sunlight as they swim around the banks of coral. Many of these have unusual shapes and are decorated with stripes, spots, and splashes of color. Larger fish, such as sharks and barracudas, usually swim in deeper water.

Many different shellfish and crabs also live in the sea. Along the coasts there are numerous kinds of sea birds, such as gulls and boobies.

On land live many kinds of snakes and lizards, toads and frogs, numerous insects, such as butterflies, cockroaches, and mosquitoes, as well as spiders of all shapes and sizes. The only kind of wildlife that the Caribbean does not have in large numbers is mammals. There are rats and mice, bats and mongooses, but no large mammals living wild.

Hibiscus

Food and trumpet
This large seashell is called a conch (usually pronounced "conk"). The shellfish that lives inside it is very tasty to eat. In many of the islands conches are used as a trumpet. An eerie honking sound can be made by blowing into the shell from one end.

The flame tree

One of the most startling sights in the Caribbean is the Royal Poinciana. It is also known as the "flame tree," or "flamboyant tree," because of its display of red flowers.

The smallest birds

Hummingbirds are the smallest birds in the world, often as small as 2 inches from beak to tail and weighing less than 2 ounces. They are called hummingbirds because their wings make a humming sound as they hover beside flowers to feed on the nectar.

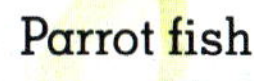

Parrots and butterflies

Many tropical fish have strange names, as a result of their extraordinary shapes and colors. There are triggerfish, parrot fish, butterfly fish, angelfish, spadefish, balloonfish, and even Puddingwives and sergeant majors.

CARIB LANDS

In the distant past, perhaps some 5,000 years ago, the Caribbean islands were occupied by small groups of Indians known as Ciboneys. About 3,000 years later, in around the 1st century AD, Arawak Indians from the northeastern regions of South America arrived and settled in the islands.

The Arawaks were peaceful people who lived by farming and traveled from island to island in dugout canoes. They grew maize (sweetcorn) and root vegetables such as cassava and sweet potatoes. They lived in simple wooden huts, made pottery and woven cloth, lay in hammocks and smoked tobacco.

Much fiercer Carib Indians started to raid the southern islands from South America in about the 14th century, gradually moving north. They attacked and killed the Arawaks, keeping their women as their wives. These were not farming people, but hunters and fishermen.

The first Europeans reached these islands in the late 15th century. In the centuries that followed, almost all the Indians died out.

KEY FACTS

▶ The Europeans called the Caribbean islands the West Indies because when they first landed they mistakenly believed they had arrived in India. Later the term "Caribbean" was also used, after the Carib Indians.

▶ A number of English words come from the languages of the Arawak and Carib Indians: *potato, maize, tobacco, canoe, hurricane, barbecue, cannibal,* and *cassava*.

▶ The name Jamaica comes from the Arawak word *Xaymaca*, meaning "land of wood and water."

▶ All the Arawaks had died out within 50 years of the arrival of the Europeans.

▶ The Caribs lived on in many islands, such as St. Lucia, St. Vincent, and Grenada, until the late 18th century, but were eventually forced out, killed, or enslaved.

Hammocks and tobacco
The first Europeans to reach the Caribbean had never seen hammocks or tobacco before. The Indians used to roll up a leaf of tobacco and smoke it through their nostrils. Cigarettes originated with the Indians of the Caribbean.

Fierce resistance

The first meetings between the Europeans and the Caribbean Indians were sometimes friendly and sometimes hostile. However, the Europeans wanted slaves and land. They also wanted the gold they had heard rumors about and were eventually to find in large quantities farther west in Central and South America. They were prepared to fight and kill to have them.

Wars between Europeans and Carib Indians lasted for three centuries. In this picture a European artist has depicted one of the first battles between the Indians and Columbus.

Christopher Columbus

Christopher Columbus led the first European expedition to the Caribbean. He was born in Genoa in Italy in 1451, but the Spanish Queen Isabella paid for his expeditions. The first island that he reached, in 1492, was Guanahani in the Bahamas, which he renamed San Salvador. In the four expeditions that he made in the next 10 years he visited most of the Caribbean islands as well as Central and South America.

Canoes

The word *canoe* comes from the Arawak language. These boats were hewn out of the single trunk of a tree, and hence were called dugouts. Small fishing craft like this one are still made in some parts of the Caribbean.

EUROPEAN SETTLERS

The Spanish were the first European settlers in the larger islands of the Greater Antilles. However, they were more interested in Central and South America, where the kingdoms of the Maya and Aztecs could provide them with huge quantities of gold. When the Spanish ships, laden with these treasures, headed back to Spain, they attracted pirates from other European countries who hid among the smaller islands ready to attack. The Caribbean became a lawless region where great fortunes were made and many lives were lost.

Meanwhile, the governments of the European countries, particularly Spain, France, England, and Holland, began to claim islands for themselves. This led to centuries of squabbles and wars. St. Lucia changed hands between the French and English 14 times before finally becoming British in 1803.

European settlers came to the islands to farm, fish, and trade. Tobacco, cotton, and ginger were the most important crops. The Dutch also traded in salt extracted from the sea water. Rich landowners employed poor laborers from Europe to work for them on their large estates on the islands. So these small, sunny outposts of Europe grew, resembling the homelands of the settlers in many ways.

Buccaneers
Throughout the Caribbean, pirates raided ships carrying gold and other valuable goods between South America and Europe. They became known as "buccaneers," a word derived from the way the pirates used the Indian method to smoke, or *boucane*, meat.

War and skirmishes
European nations fought fiercely over many of the Caribbean islands. These nations were frequently at war with each other during the centuries following Columbus' arrival on the islands. Whoever had the most sea power usually won the fight. This picture shows a British ship taking on a Spanish galleon in the year 1743.

Europe in the sun

Many of the older towns of the Caribbean were built like European cities. These old houses in Willemstad, Curaçao, were built by the Dutch in the same style as their buildings back home in Holland.

Spanish colonies

The first Spanish settlers in the Caribbean built mighty fortresses to protect their colonies and their gold from attack. The first Spanish colony was at Santo Domingo, now the capital of the Dominican Republic. It has a magnificent cathedral, built between 1512 and 1540 (shown here).

GRIM TRAFFIC

Sugar changed the history of the Caribbean. Sugar cane grows only in a warm climate. Before settling the Caribbean, Europeans had consumed small amounts of sugar, from sugar cane grown in the Mediterranean region and later in Madeira and the Canary Islands. Now they could grow their own cane, and could be supplied with huge quantities of sugar to satisfy their ever-increasing desire for sweet food.

Large numbers of people were needed to work on the plantations that grew the sugar cane. Black African slaves had been imported to the Caribbean by the Spanish as early as 1510. By the mid-17th century, 150 years later, they were being imported and sold throughout the Caribbean in vast numbers. Landowners found it was cheaper to buy and keep a slave than to employ a European laborer under contract.

The slaves came from western Africa, where local slave dealers collected them and sold them to European slave traders. They were transported in ships across the Atlantic, and then sold to the Spanish, French, and British landowners in the Caribbean.

The overseer
It was the overseer's job to keep the slaves working. This was usually achieved with a whip. Slaves were provided with clothing, huts to live in, and enough food to keep them alive.

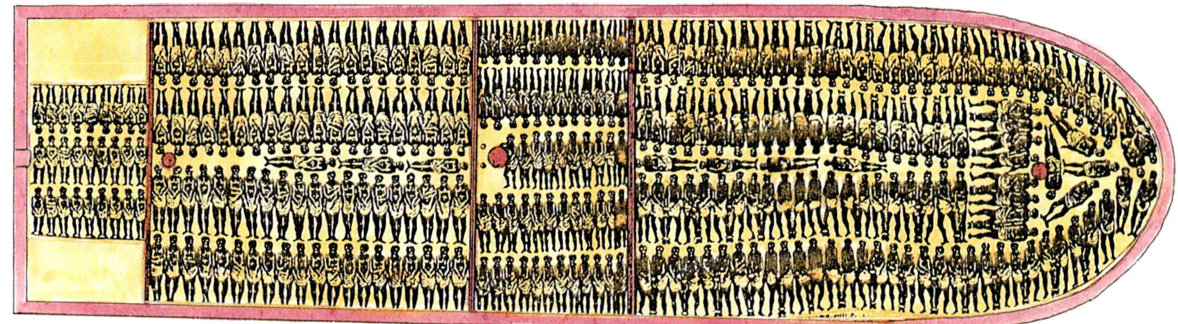

Human cargo
Conditions in the slave ships were appalling. The slaves were shackled to the deck, lying side by side, with no access to fresh air. The slave traders wanted to get as many slaves to the islands as possible, as cheaply as possible.

KEY FACTS

- About 15 million slaves were taken from Africa to North and South America and the Caribbean between 1510 and 1865. Slaves numbering 750,000 were taken to Jamaica alone.
- The mid-17th century saw the most dramatic increase in slave traffic. In 1629 there were about 50 slaves in Barbados, but by 1673 there were 30,000.
- Up to a quarter of the slaves on the slave ships died along the way.
- Portugal, Holland, and Great Britain were the main nations that transported and traded in slaves.
- The British banned the use of slave labor in 1833, and the French in 1848. Cuba was the last island to give up slavery, in 1886.

Rich rewards
Landowners with large sugar plantations became very wealthy and built grand houses on their estates. Some of these houses still survive and have been converted into hotels for tourists. This is the Plantation Leyritz in Martinique.

Sugar cane
Sugar cane grows from cuttings in about 16 months, when it is harvested and sent to a factory to be crushed to extract the sweet juice. Sugar is made by boiling this juice. Cane-cutting is hard and unpleasant work in the hot, tropical sun. The cane leaves are sharp, and there are frequent accidents with the razor-sharp machetes used to cut the stalks of sugar cane.

REVOLT AND FREEDOM

The conditions in which slaves worked and lived were so appalling that landowners realized slaves might break into violent revolt at any time. Slave owners did what they could to prevent this, and punishments for rebellion were severe.

Despite this, revolts did take place. One successful rebellion in the French colony of St. Domingue was led by a slave, Toussaint L'Ouverture. St. Domingue then became the first independent Caribbean nation, returning to its old Arawak name, Haiti.

When slavery ended in the 19th century, conditions for many of the freed slaves actually became worse. Landowners brought in laborers from China and India to replace their slave work forces. Many of the ex-slaves now had no work and no land to live on. Those who did work earned very little. Extreme poverty was common.

It has been a long and sometimes violent struggle between the Caribbean islanders and their colonial masters. Only in this century have most of the Caribbean islands been allowed to choose how they are governed. Many have chosen to be independent.

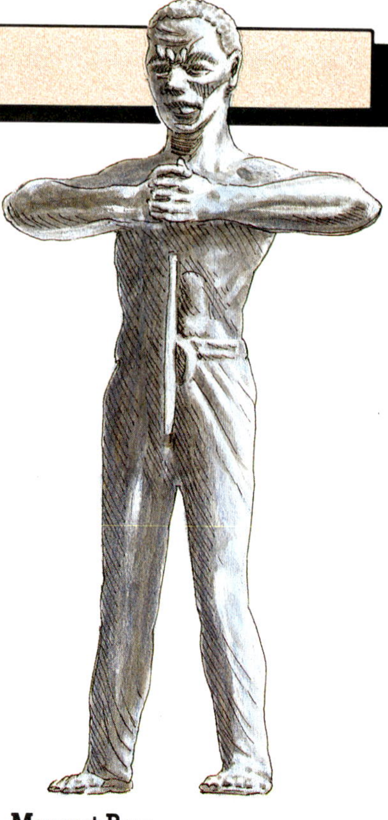

Morant Bay
In 1865 in Morant Bay, Jamaica, a large group of blacks, some of them former slaves, rose up in rebellion because of their poverty. The British colonial authorities reacted harshly. Four hundred and thirty-nine rioters (including the leaders, Paul Bogle and George William Gordon) were executed, and 600 prisoners were flogged. This statue of Paul Bogle is in Spanish Town, Jamaica.

Life today
In the 20th century Caribbean islanders are their own masters, although for many people unemployment and a low standard of living are still problems.

Indians from India

Large numbers of Indians and Chinese came to the Caribbean when slavery ended. They worked for low wages on contracts lasting a number of years. Many stayed on after their contracts ended. Over a third of the population of Trinidad today is of Asian origin. This is because Trinidad only began large-scale sugar production after slavery had been abolished. Therefore, they had to import a large labor force.

Slave hero

Toussaint L'Ouverture was born a slave in Haiti (then called St. Domingue) in about 1743. When a group of slaves rebelled in the 1780s he joined them in their mountain hideout, soon becoming their leader. In 1791 he led 500,000 slaves in a revolt against the French landowners, and in 1794 the slaves were declared free. Toussaint became governor of St. Domingue and a general in the French army. However, the French wanted to take back their colony and tricked Toussaint into capture. He died in a French prison in 1803, but the fight continued. A year later Haiti became independent.

IN THE SHADOW OF THE PAST

The Caribbean's harsh and difficult history has left many scars. Millions of people were brought to these islands as slaves. They lived in dreadful conditions. Although the people who owned them were making a lot of money through the profits sugar brought, they did not pass on any of this profit to the slaves. However, the sugar industry has declined. Most of the islands now have far greater populations than they can provide for. There is not enough work for everybody, and not enough money to go around. Most of the people of the Caribbean are very poorly paid.

On many of the islands people lead simple lives, which have hardly changed for generations. They grow vegetables on small plots of land, rear a few chickens, cows, and goats, and fish in small boats. In this way they may be able to provide enough for their families.

However, for many years now people have been leaving the countryside for the towns, especially the capital cities, in search of work. The result is that many of the towns are overcrowded. Housing and services, such as water supply, buses, and hospitals, are stretched to the breaking point.

These conditions caused large numbers of people to leave the Caribbean islands during the 1950s and 1960s in search of better prospects abroad. Most of these people settled in the United States, Canada, and Great Britain.

KEY FACTS

▶ Unemployment in many Caribbean islands is very high. About a third of Jamaica's work force is unemployed.

▶ The Caribbean once supplied most of Europe's sugar; now Europe gets most of its sugar from sugar beet, which it grows itself.

▶ In many of the islands, such as Cuba, Jamaica, St. Vincent, Antigua, Grenada and St. Lucia, over a quarter of the total population live in and around the capital city.

▶ During the 1950s and early 1960s about 10,000 people left the Caribbean every year to settle in Great Britain; during the same period about 45,000 Puerto Ricans emigrated to the United States every year.

▶ Anguilla has a population of 6,500, but there are about 20,000 Anguillans now living in other parts of the world.

Daily catch
Fishing is still a very important way of providing food throughout the region. Fishermen go out in small boats, built in traditional style, and use nets to catch fish.

Traditions of hardship

People in many parts of the Caribbean live in shacks made of just enough wood and corrugated iron to keep the rain out. This is a shanty town on the edge of Kingston, Jamaica.

Pride in the past

Many aspects of plantation life are reflected in folk tales, traditional dancing, and costumes. This woman is wearing the traditional costume of Martinique, which shows both African and European influences.

Emigration

During the 1950s and 1960s Great Britain encouraged large numbers of people from the English-speaking islands to settle in Great Britain, where they were needed to work. These people arrived with high hopes for the future, but were often disappointed.

THE CHOICE OF GOVERNMENT

The Caribbean today is searching for solutions to its many problems. These islands are not rich enough to survive on their own. They depend on overseas trade, on tourism, and on their political relationships with other countries.

Some of the smaller islands have chosen to remain colonies, or dependencies, of a European country. For example, the Cayman Islands are a dependent territory of Great Britain. Puerto Rico has a close relationship with the United States. Puerto Ricans are U.S. citizens and can work here. Other islands are independent, but usually have a close association with Europe or the United States, or, in the case of Cuba, with the Soviet Union. Most countries have elected governments, although Cuba has a communist government and Haiti's government is controlled by the army.

The Caribbean countries have not joined together as European countries, for example, have done. The Federation of the West Indies was formed, but did not last long. Former British islands are part of the British Commonwealth and have formed CARICOM, the Caribbean Community and Common Market, to promote trade within the islands. However, in general, there is not a great sense of unity among these islands.

Fidel Castro
Fidel Castro has been Cuba's leader since 1958, when he led a communist rebellion against the corrupt government of Fulgencio Batista. With help from the Soviet Union, Cuba has managed to solve many of the typical problems of the Caribbean. Everyone has a job, there is good health care and education, but the people must accept the strict control of the government.

A colony by choice
The Turks and Caicos Islands are a British Crown colony. They have a British governor who takes his instructions from London. Many aspects of the administration, including the courts and the police force, retain strong British traditions. The currency of the islands, however, is the U.S. dollar.

Invasion

The United States takes a great interest in the Caribbean because it is so close. It wants only friendly nations on its doorstep. During the early 1980s, Grenada was building strong links with the communists in Cuba. When the prime minister of Grenada was assassinated by rival communist leaders in 1983, the United States decided to intervene, to restore an elected government. U.S. marines, assisted by troops from the islands of the eastern Caribbean and Jamaica, landed in Grenada and defeated the communists. The troops withdrew and a new prime minister was elected.

France in the Caribbean

Guadeloupe and Martinique are two French islands in the Caribbean. In 1946 they became departments of France and are treated as though they are a part of France. They send their own elected representatives to the French parliament in Paris.

A FUTURE IN INDUSTRY

One of the ways that the Caribbean is improving its prospects for the future is through industry. A number of islands, particularly Puerto Rico, are increasing their light industry. They are building factories to produce electrical goods, textiles and clothing, plastics, sports equipment, and medicines.

The Greater Antilles are rich in minerals, and Cuba produces iron, copper, manganese, and chrome. Jamaica produces large quantities of bauxite, which is used to make aluminum. Trinidad has oil, and oil refineries, which make it one of the wealthiest islands in the region. There are also oil refineries in Curaçao, Bonaire, Aruba, and St. Croix in the U.S. Virgin Islands. These refineries process oil imported from Venezuela and the Middle East.

This growing industry has helped to provide the money to build better roads and to improve telephone systems. Shipping is of vital importance to the islands. They depend on ships for importing and exporting goods in bulk. The Caribbean ports also serve ships traveling between the Atlantic and Pacific oceans through the Panama Canal in Central America. A number of modern ports and terminals have been built in the Caribbean in recent years.

On the rig
Oil has been produced in Trinidad since 1909. In the 1950s oil rigs like the one shown here were set up in the sea, off the coasts of Trinidad. In the 1970s Trinidad started to produce natural gas as well.

Refining oil
The Shell Oil Refinery in Curaçao is a massive complex that attracts workers from all over the region. Another Caribbean oil refinery, on St. Croix in the U.S. Virgin Islands, is the largest refinery in the world, producing more than 300,000 barrels a day.

Industrial Trinidad
With the benefit of income from its oil, Trinidad has been able to invest heavily in industry, making it the Caribbean's most industrialized nation. This factory assembles cars from kits that are imported from Japan.

Bauxite
Jamaica is the world's third largest producer of bauxite, after Australia and Guinea (in Africa). Bauxite is used to make aluminum. But because this process requires a great deal of electricity, Jamaica exports most of its bauxite as alumina, a white powder that can then be turned into aluminum. This factory is in Ocho Rios, Jamaica.

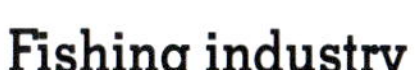

Fishing industry
Cuba is the only Caribbean country to make the most of fishing as an industry. It has a fleet of large, modern fishing vessels that work across the Atlantic.

TROPICAL BLISS

Tourism is now the single most important source of income for almost all the Caribbean countries. Millions of tourists come to the Caribbean, mainly from the United States and Europe, and usually during the winter months in search of sun and warmth.

The Caribbean is ideal for tourism, with its beautiful islands, sandy beaches, and first-class hotels. The atmosphere is generally friendly and welcoming. Visitors can enjoy all kinds of water sports, such as scuba-diving and water-skiing, they can visit historic forts and plantations, or simply relax on the beach.

The tourist industry needs large numbers of people to run the hotels and restaurants, the bus services, airports, and shops. This gives local people jobs. It also brings money to the governments of the islands. This money can then be spent on improving the airports and roads and other services that tourists use, as well as on schools and hospitals for the islanders.

The development of tourism has to be carefully planned, however. Beautiful beaches can be ruined if too many hotels are built too quickly. And if the money that comes from tourism is not distributed fairly among local people, resentment and bitterness can result.

A welcoming smile
The tourist industry now employs large numbers of people throughout the region. Many of the hotel employees have been professionally trained, and provide a very high standard of service.

Cruising
The Caribbean is a favorite destination for cruise ships, which take visitors from island to island. Unfortunately, these tourists spend little time on shore. Therefore, they do not bring in much income for the islanders.

Beautiful beaches
The Caribbean has many fine beaches, such as this one at Pidgeon Point, Tobago. Many luxurious hotels, attracting tourists, have been built all over the Caribbean, often with money invested from abroad. Caribbean governments have to be careful that all the profits from such developments do not go abroad as well.

KEY FACTS

- ▶ Two million tourists visit the Bahamas every year, 10 for every member of the Bahamian population.
- ▶ The tourist industry of the Bahamas employs two-thirds of the work force.
- ▶ More than a million tourists now visit Jamaica every year.
- ▶ Nearly three-quarters of the income of the Cayman Islands comes from tourism.
- ▶ Many tourists in the Caribbean spend in two days what the average Haitian earns in one year.
- ▶ Two-thirds of the visitors to the Virgin Islands stay on yachts.

A yachting paradise?
The Caribbean provides a wonderful setting for yacht owners. In recent years, though, modern-day pirates have been known to operate around some of the islands, robbing the yachts.

MAKING THE MOST OF THE LAND

Agriculture still plays a very important role in the Caribbean. The more food that each island can produce for itself, the less it has to bring in from abroad. Several agricultural products are important exports.

Bananas and coconuts are grown throughout the region. The eastern islands, particularly Montserrat and Barbados, grow a very fine kind of cotton called Sea Island cotton. Spices, such as nutmeg, cinnamon, and allspice, are an important product of Grenada. A famous type of coffee called Blue Mountain comes from Jamaica. St. Vincent produces arrowroot, which is used as a thickener in cooking. Cuba grows tobacco to make cigars, which are considered to be the best in the world.

Cattle-ranching for beef has become big business in the Dominican Republic and Cuba, while dairy farming is important in Puerto Rico.

A number of research laboratories have been set up in the region to study the problems facing farmers in the Caribbean, and to discover new strains of plants and new breeds of farm animals that will be suited to the soil and climate.

KEY FACTS

- ▶ Martinique and Guadeloupe are the islands that produce the most bananas in the Caribbean. However, the Caribbean only produces one-tenth of the world's bananas.
- ▶ Exporting bananas has only been possible in this century, when refrigerated ships were invented.
- ▶ The Caribbean produces about a quarter of the world's sugar.
- ▶ Cuba produces more sugar than the rest of the islands in the Caribbean put together.
- ▶ The Dominican Republic is the largest producer of coffee in the Caribbean.
- ▶ One of the region's highest earning agricultural products is the illegal drug cannabis (marijuana is made from this herb). Some 2,000 tons of this, valued at nearly $200 million, are smuggled into the United States every year.

Bananas!
Banana trees grow everywhere in the Caribbean. The bananas grow on long, hanging stems in clumps of 50 or more. If the bananas are to be exported, they are picked while they are still green, to be ripened later.

World-famous cigars

The best Cuban cigars, often called Havanas after the Cuban capital, are still made by hand.

On the ranch

Cattle-ranching has become increasingly important in the Caribbean, especially on the larger islands. New breeds of cattle have been developed that are well adapted to the Caribbean climate.

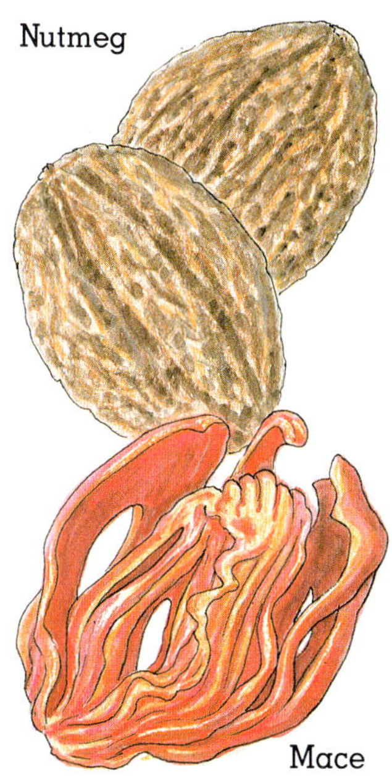

The Spice Island

This is the name given to Grenada, which produces large quantities of spices, such as mace and nutmeg. The spice trees originally came from Indonesian islands, which were once the only places in the world where such valuable spices could be grown.

RICE AND PEAS

Caribbean cooking is a tasty mixture of South American, European, African, and Indian food, often spiced with hot chili peppers. There are lots of things to eat in the Caribbean, such as fish, crabs and lobster, a huge range of tropical fruit, chicken, beef, and goat meat.

Root vegetables play an important role in the Caribbean diet. Cassava, once grown by the Arawak Indians, is cooked as a vegetable or made into flour or tapioca. Yams and taro came from Africa and are eaten like potatoes. The taro plant also produces spinach-like leaves called callaloo.

Other Caribbean specialities make use of the nutty-flavored West Indian pumpkin and the pear-shaped, watery vegetable called christophene or cho-cho. Meat and vegetables can be cooked with coconut milk or limes, mangoes or green bananas, often with a touch of Indian curry spices.

For everyday meals people often eat a little fish or meat, sometimes cooked in a stew with vegetables, and accompanied by fried plantain bananas and "rice and peas" — rice served with fried red kidney beans.

Natural sweetness
Raw cane juice can make a refreshing, sweet drink. It is sold in the streets, and is crushed from the cane while you wait. Or, if you prefer, you can simply suck on a piece of raw cane!

Fruit of the *Bounty*
Breadfruit, pictured at the left, grows on trees and is cooked as a vegetable. It has a starchy flavor, a little like that of a potato. The breadfruit tree originally came from the Pacific Ocean, and was brought to the Caribbean by an English naval officer named Captain Bligh. The first time he tried to make this journey, in 1789, the men of his ship, HMS *Bounty*, mutinied against his harsh discipline.

Market day

Traders and people with small farms bring their fruit and vegetables to the local markets to sell. These colorful markets are usually run by women and are similar in many ways to West African markets.

Tropical fruits

All these fruits are grown in the Caribbean. The coconut is shown as it grows on the tree, before the thick, green, outer husk is removed.

Saltfish and ackee

This is one of the famous dishes of the Caribbean, particularly Jamaica. Ackee is the fruit of a tree that originally came from Africa. When cooked, it tastes like scrambled eggs. Other ingredients include fish (usually salted cod from Canada or Scandinavia), onions, chili peppers, salt pork, and the herb thyme. It's delicious for breakfast!

RELIGIOUS STRENGTH

By far the most important religion in the Caribbean is Christianity. The majority of Christians there belong to the Roman Catholic Church. Many of the islanders are deeply religious, and go to church at least once a week. Those who are not Catholics belong to the Protestant churches.

However, people of most of the world's religions live in the Caribbean. There are about 300,000 Hindus and 75,000 Muslims in Trinidad, and a number of Jews throughout the islands.

Some Caribbean people follow religions that originally came from Africa with the slaves and now also include elements of Christianity. Pocomania, which is practiced by some people in Jamaica, is one of these. Rastafarianism, which developed in Jamaica during this century, is another.

Voodoo is a religion that involves African gods, witchcraft, and spells, and voodoo priests are said to be able to speak to the dead. It is widely practiced in Haiti — officially a Roman Catholic country — and is found in various forms in many other parts of the Caribbean.

Rastafarians
Rastafarianism takes its name from its figurehead, the former African emperor of Ethiopia, Haile Selassie (1892-1975), who as a prince was called Ras Tafari. Rastafarians believe their religion can free them from a world of evil. They are distinguished by their "dreadlocks" — the style of their long hair.

Churchgoers
Many Caribbean children go to Sunday School, and sing in church choirs. Adults go to church regularly. Most of the churches in the Caribbean have been built in traditional European style.

A piece of Paris
This splendid church, set in the hills of Martinique, is a copy of the church called the Sacré Coeur, which stands on a hill in Paris, France.

Mosques and temples
The Asian population of Trinidad gives the island the highest non-Christian population in the Caribbean. The Hindus worship at temples; the Muslims, at mosques. This is a Hindu temple in Trinidad.

HEALTHY AND WISE

The Caribbean children of today will have the future of the islands in their hands when they grow up. Most of the Caribbean countries have given a lot of attention to their schools. The standard of education was often very high while the islands were ruled by European countries, and in many cases these standards have been kept up by governments and teachers. In most islands education is free from the age of 5 to 16. After that a student might go on to a technical college or a university, such as the University of the West Indies, which has colleges in Jamaica, Trinidad, and Barbados.

There are many good doctors and hospitals in the Caribbean. However, both hospitals and schools are expensive to build and to run. Many of the Caribbean countries cannot afford to provide the same kind of health and education facilities found in Europe or the United States.

In the poorer rural areas, school buildings are sometimes just simple wooden huts with benches and a chalkboard. The people in these areas rely on local doctors and folk medicine when they are ill.

School for grownups
Many of the islands run classes for adults. Some older people did not have the chance to go to school when they were young, so they take the opportunity to learn in later life.

Going to school in shifts

Children in most Caribbean countries wear school uniforms. In many places, because there are not enough schools, children go to school in shifts. Some children go in the morning, and some in the afternoon.

The Cuban example

Cuba has the best health and educational facilities in the Caribbean. Through public programs in health and hygiene in the past 30 years, many serious diseases, such as diptheria and polio, have been brought under control. The people now live longer, healthier lives. The young Cubans shown here are training to become doctors.

SPORTS AND LEISURE

Most Caribbean schools include sports in their daily activities. People interested in sports can begin to develop their talents while still at school. Several of the islands send teams to the Olympic Games and have provided some celebrated medal-winners, particularly in athletics.

The sports played by the various islands reflect those traditionally played by the countries that ruled them in the past. The former Spanish and American islands, for example, play baseball and basketball. The former British islands play cricket. People follow the progress of their national sports teams with great interest and enthusiasm.

For the most part, the Caribbean islanders like to enjoy life, spending their free time on the beach, relaxing and talking with friends over a cool drink, playing cards or dominoes, going out to the movies, or just staying at home to watch the television or listen to the radio.

Gold-medal athlete
Don Quarrie is one of the great athletes of Jamaica. He won the 200-meter gold medal and 100-meter silver medal at the 1976 Olympic Games, held in Montreal, Canada. He holds the record for winning the most gold medals in the Commonwealth Games.

Cricketing hero
The West Indian cricket team is made up of players from the various former British islands. They have included some of the greatest cricket players of all time. This is Viv Richards, one of cricket's greatest batsmen.

Slapping them down

Dominoes is usually thought of as a quiet, restful game. But this is not so in the Caribbean. Games are often played with resounding bangs and crashes as the dominoes are slapped down on the table, accompanied by the excited cries of spectators.

Enjoying the Caribbean

The people of the Caribbean islands enjoy the sun, the sea, and the landscape of the islands as much as any tourist does. Swimming is a popular activity, especially on weekends. This is the Dunn's River Falls in Jamaica, a popular place for swimming.

CARIBBEAN RHYTHMS

Two of the most popular pastimes in the Caribbean are music and dancing. At parties or festivals, and even at some church services, all kinds of people, from the youngest to the oldest, can be seen dancing or just gently swaying to the rhythms of the music.

Caribbean music has its roots in Africa, Europe, and South America, but the mixture has a character all its own. It ranges from the lively and carefully written songs of the calypso singers of Trinidad to reggae from Jamaica — a kind of rock music that has a special guitar beat echoed by the drums. Salsa, music and singing set to a breathtaking rhythm, is a speciality of Puerto Rico. Soca music (short for "soul calypso") is a blend of calypso-style singing with salsa-like rhythms. New styles of music are being invented all the time.

Caribbean music has become famous throughout the world, and in recent years music has developed into an important industry. The stars of reggae, soca, and salsa music make tours abroad and sell millions of records. In several of the islands there are modern recording studios run by international companies. These companies bring large sums of money to the Caribbean. Music has become big business.

King of reggae
The Jamaican singer Bob Marley was the greatest star of reggae music, traveling around the world with his band, The Wailers. His career was cut short when he died of cancer in 1981.

Styles of the past
Some traditional Caribbean dancing has grown out of the formal styles of European ballroom dancing of the past, but with its own quite distinctive flavor. These people from Martinique are dancing the "beguine."

"Play mas"

"Play mas" means "have fun at the carnival." Carnivals take place on many of the Caribbean islands, usually during the few days before Lent begins (40 days before Easter). It is a time for celebration, with music, dancing, and fantastic costumes. The carnival in Trinidad shown here is the most spectacular of the Caribbean.

The music of oil drums

Steel bands were invented in Trinidad. The tops of empty oil drums are carefully beaten with hammers into segments so that each area will produce a different sound.

THE CARIBBEAN EYE

The history of the Caribbean and the way of life today have given the Caribbean people their unique outlook on the world. They have been brought up on these islands in close-knit communities surrounded by a rich and colorful landscape. But often they have also experienced the problems of poverty.

Caribbean painting and writing reflect the people's outlook. There are many painters throughout the islands, many of whom live by selling their work to tourists. They often use bright colors and bold figures to portray the beauty that can be found in everyday Caribbean life.

Poems and novels from the Caribbean often express the hardships of life there, and the difficulties that face people of the islands who have gone to live abroad. Many writers make use of the languages of their own island, especially creole or patois. These languages, which have developed in the islands from a mixture of European and African languages, are now seen as having a beauty and strength of their own.

Increasingly the people of the Caribbean are learning to value the special qualities of their culture. They are making efforts to ensure that in a rapidly changing world their traditional language, folk tales, and art are not lost.

Caribbean words
The work of many Caribbean writers is now widely read. One of the most popular is George Lamming, who was born in Barbados in 1927. His famous novel *In the Castle of My Skin*, with its portrait of childhood in the West Indies, was first published in 1953.

Images of Africa
Caribbean sculptors use fine hardwoods that come from the forests of the larger islands and from Central America. Their work often reflects traditional West African sculpture.

Practical crafts

Local Caribbean crafts include jewelry made from coral and shells; pottery; embroidery; and hats and baskets made from cane, bamboo, and palm leaves.

The colors of the sun

Caribbean painters often use a bright range of colors to portray the vivid landscape and clothing of the islands. The art of Haiti is probably the best known, and consists of pictures of everyday Haitian life painted with a special, joyous charm.

FAMILY LIFE

Peter lives in Sauteurs, in the north of the island of Grenada. The quiet, pleasant little town has a French name because the island was French before it became British in 1783. The name means "jumpers," because Carib Indians jumped to their deaths from cliffs near there rather than surrender to the French.

Peter lives with his family in an old wooden house by the road. It is not much, but it keeps the rain out. It has a wonderful verandah with bougainvillea flowers spilling down from the roof. Peter spends a lot of time with his grandmother; she's at home when he gets back from school at lunchtime. His mother works at the spice farm down the road. His father works at the harbor at St. George's, the island's capital, a long bus journey away. His older sister works at a hotel on the Grand Anse beach near St. George's. Peter would also like to work in a hotel, but he will have to wait a while. He is only 10 and has another five years of school.

Peter has lots of friends and they play football and go swimming in the sea together. Soon it will be the school holidays. Peter's uncle and aunt and cousins are coming over from London to visit. Then there will be a real party!

Grandmothers
Grandmothers play an important part in the life of Caribbean children. Fathers are often away at work, or abroad, or may not live with the family at all. Many mothers work. So grandmothers often bring up the children.

Getting around

The majority of families in the Caribbean do not have a car of their own, but there is usually good bus service all over the islands. Some of these buses are minibuses; others are old coaches that rattle around the countryside. There are also new, air-conditioned luxury buses.

Home

Many of the older houses in the Caribbean are small wooden buildings raised above the ground on stilts. The one real enemy of these houses is hurricanes, which can easily destroy them. In Hurricane Gilbert in 1988 four out of five houses in Jamaica lost their roofs.

THE FUTURE

The Caribbean now has much better prospects for the future than it used to have. Tourism has been important, bringing millions of dollars to the islands every year. This has provided money to improve roads, housing, schools, and hospitals. It has given jobs to millions of people who might otherwise have gone abroad in search of work, as many Caribbean people have had to do in the past.

The countries of the Caribbean, however, know that they cannot depend on tourism alone. What would happen if tourists stopped coming to the Caribbean? Many of the islands have been careful to use their income to build up industries and to train their people in new skills so that tourism won't be the only source of jobs and money. However, development is coming slowly.

The Caribbean has a particular charm of its own. The islanders are anxious to ensure that they keep this special charm as they move forward to face the future.

Modern shopping
Not long ago most islanders did their shopping at small stores, groceries, and markets. Now, however, supermarkets are fairly common in most parts of the Caribbean, providing a wide range of goods from all over the world.

The old and the new
A modern bus in the streets of Havana, Cuba's capital. In the background are buildings from Cuba's colonial past. Cuba allowed these buildings to fall into decay, but is now beginning to restore them as historical monuments.

Tax havens

Many of the islands are encouraging foreign companies to bring money to them, either for investing in industry or just for banking. Some, such as the Cayman Islands and the Turks and Caicos Islands, offer special tax arrangements that make it cheaper for companies to register there. The islands receive large incomes from providing this service. This is the marina on the aptly-named Paradise Island in the Bahamas, a tax haven for many British tax payers.

Old-fashioned charm

This attractive old house, built in traditional style with its shutters and verandah, provides a reminder of the values of the past.

Modernization

San Juan, the capital of Puerto Rico, has undergone a massive building boom in recent years, making it the most modern city of the region. Hotels, office buildings, and apartments now form an impressive skyline, with a network of highways feeding into the city.

Index

Acknowledgments

Map illustrations (pages 6-7) by Ann Savage.
All other illustrations by Borin van Loon.
Photographic credits (*a* = above, *b* = below, *m* = middle, *l* = left, *r* = right): Cover *al* Robert Harding Picture Library, *bl* Zefa, *ar* Robert Harding Picture Library, *br* Zefa; Page 8 Philip Wolmuth/Hutchison Library; page 9 Robert Harding Picture Library; page 11 Zefa; page 15 *a* Robert Harding Picture Library, *b* Bernard Régent/Hutchison Library; page 17 Antony Mason; page 18 Christine Pemberton/Hutchison Library; page 19 Michael Friedel/Rex Features; page 21 Popperfoto; page 22 Fieter Ludwig/Sipa Press/Rex Features; page 23 Bernard Régent/Hutchison Library; page 25 *r* Robert Harding Picture Library, *l* Philip Wolmuth/Hutchison Library; page 27 Clive Sawyer/Zefa; page 29 *a* Christine Pemberton/Hutchison Library, *b* Kurt Scholz/Zefa; page 30 Hutchison Library; page 31 Robert Harding Picture Library; page 32 Clive Dixon/Rex Features; page 33 *a* Robert Harding Picture Library, *b* Dr Seeberg/Zefa; page 35 Robert Harding Picture Library; page 36 Adrian Murrell/Allsport; page 37 Zefa; page 38 Rex Features; page 39 *a* Robert Harding Picture Library, *b* Robert Harding Picture Library; page 41 Hutchison Library; page 43 E. Earp/Zefa; page 44 Zefa-Damm; page 45 *a* Zefa, *b* G. Ricatto/Zefa.